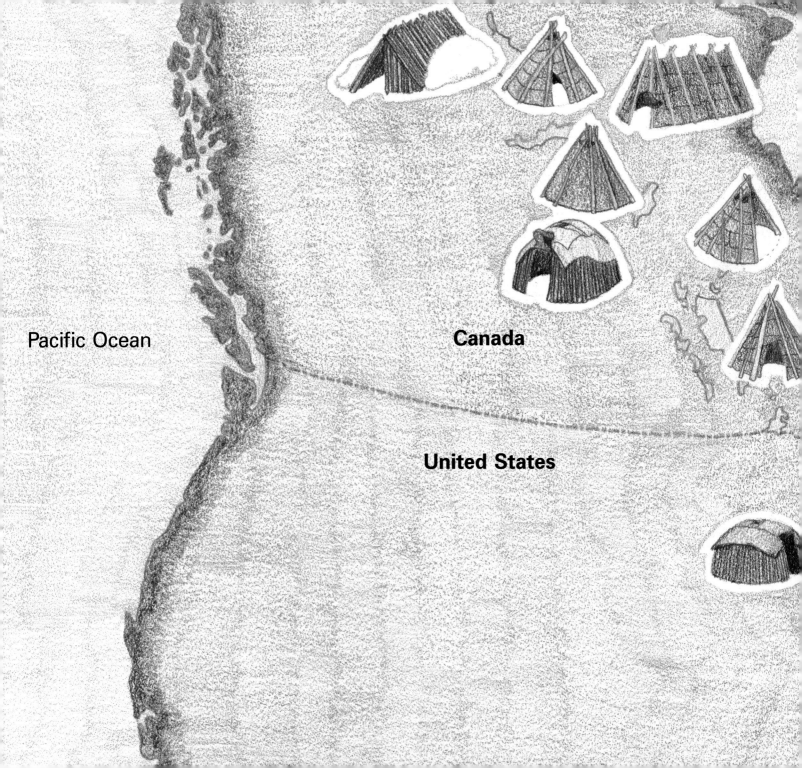

Pacific Ocean

Canada

United States

Hudson Bay

Atlantic Ocean

**Native dwellings:
woodland Indians**

Bonnie Shemie

Houses of bark

tipi, wigwam and longhouse

Tundra Books

Published in Canada by Tundra Books, Montreal, Quebec H3G 1R4
Published in the United States by Tundra Books of Northern New York, Plattsburgh, N.Y. 12901
Distributed in the United Kingdom by Ragged Bears Ltd., Andover, Hampshire SP11 9HX
Distributed in France by Le colporteur diffusion, 84100 Orange

ISBN 0-88776-246-8

Library of Congress Catalog Number: 90-70130

The publisher has applied funds from its Canada Council block grant for 1990 toward the editing and production of this book.

Canadian Cataloging in Publication Data

Shemie, Bonnie, 1949-
 Houses of bark

Also issued in a French edition: *Maisons d'écorce*
ISBN 0-88776-246-8

 1. Woodland Indians — Dwellings. I. Title.

E78.E2S34 1990 j392'.36'0089973 C90-090156-X

Printed in Hong Kong by the South China Printing Co. (1988) Ltd.

Also by Bonnie Shemie:
Houses of snow, skin and bones

Acknowledgments:
The author/illustrator would like to thank Professor Norman Clermont of the Department of Anthropology, Université de Montréal, for his generous advice, and also Norbert Schoenauer at the School of Architecture at McGill University, Montreal. She also wishes to acknowledge the help of archaeologist Charles A. Martijn from Direction du Nouveau-Québec et service aux autochtones, ministère des Affaires culturelles, Government of Quebec, Quebec; Conrad Graham and Pamela Miller of the McCord Museum of Canadian History, McGill University; Sandra Saddy at the Huronia Historical Resource Centre in Midland, Ontario; Shirley Scott of the Kahnawake Culture Centre, Kahnawake, Quebec. She would also like to thank the people of the Notman Photo Archives, McCord Museum; the Native Friendship Centre, Montreal; and the National Museums of Canada, Ottawa, for their cooperation.

Bibliography:
Ablek, Thomas S., "Longhouse and Palisade: Northeastern Iroquoian Villages of the Seventeenth Century," *The Quarterly Journal of the Ontario Historical Society*, vol. LXII, March 1970.
Claiborne, Robert, *The First Americans*. New York: Time-Life Books, 1973.
Dodd, Christine, *Ontario Iroquois Tradition Longhouses*. Ottawa: The National Museums of Canada, 1984.
Driver, Harold, *Indians of North America*. Chicago: University of Chicago Press, 1961.
Georgekish, Fred, "Studies in Habitation: Traditional Cree Construction — Paint Hills Forms," thesis for La Direction du Nord-du-Québec, ministère des Affaires culturelles, Government of Quebec, Quebec, 1979.
Jenness, Diamond, *The Indians of Canada*, 7th ed. Toronto: University of Toronto Press, 1977.
Kelly, Robert N., *The Huron Corn Planters of the Eastern Woodlands*. Toronto: Nelson (Canada), 1986.
Koerte, Arnold, *Toward the Design of Shelter Forms in the North*. Winnipeg: University of Manitoba Press, 1974.
La Farge, Oliver, *A Pictorial History of the American Indian*. New York: Crown, 1956.
Morgan, Lewis H., *Houses and House-Life of American Aborigines*. Originally published in 1881. Chicago: University of Chicago Press, 1965.
Sturtevant, William C., ed., *Handbook of North American Indians*, vols. 6 (1981) and 15 (1984). Washington: Smithsonian Institute.
Wallis, Ruth S. and Wilson D., *The Micmac Indians of Eastern Canada*. Minneapolis: University of Minnesota Press, 1955.
Warrick, Garry, *Reconstructing Ontario Iroquoian Village Organization*. Ottawa: National Museums of Canada, 1984.

2 *crooked knife with beaver-tooth blade*

The northern woodlands

In the afternoon twilight of a northern Canadian forest, far from other small Indian bands, two mothers and three small children are rushing to build a shelter. The temperature is dropping, warning of a cold night ahead, and soon the men will return from hunting. The women move quickly, hacking down small trees and cutting off branches to make poles as support for a small tipi. They have carried a bundle of bark with them, but it must be warmed and softened before it can be unrolled and wrapped around the poles. The children are sent to search for dry sticks to start a fire.

The tipi they are building may shelter the two families for as little as one night, or for as long as several weeks if the men continue to find moose. Tonight, for extra warmth, they will all grease their bodies with bear fat and tie in the sleeves of their beaver capes before going to sleep, huddled together safe from wind and snow in their little bark shelter.

This scene was common in the woodlands of north-eastern Canada as recently as a hundred years ago. But farther south on both sides of the Canada-United States border six hundred years earlier, Indians were building far grander structures. Where tribes were able to grow corn they did not have to move in a continual search for food; they built longhouses sometimes large enough to shelter a hundred people for as long as fifteen years.

What both Indian structures — the tiniest tipi and the largest longhouse — had in common was the material used to build them. Wherever there were forests, there was some kind of bark: birch, cedar, spruce, elm, basswood, ash and oak. It was simple to cut, light to carry and easy to work with. It was used as food, clothing and medicine. Waterproof, it could be made into containers for drinking and cooking, for carrying or storing, and into canoes for traveling. But most ingenious of all was the way it was used to make shelters.

3

Forests spreading from the Yukon southeast to Virginia provided all the bark

5

needed to build native shelters: tipi, wigwam, and even the vast longhouse.

The bark tipi

The forests of northern Canada were once rich in animal life and the Indians who lived by hunting moved often as they followed the herds. The tipi of bark became the common shelter.

The search for usable bark went on all year round. When families passed through forests and noticed trees with good bark, they stripped off the lower branches. New bark would grow over the holes leaving the trunk smooth. Birchbark was preferred over all other kinds because it came off the trees in larger strips and was lighter to carry.

Bark requires careful handling or it splits. There was a precise time in the spring when it was best for peeling. As the sheets were cut and stripped from the trees, they were stretched flat on the ground and weighed down with stones. Rows of star-shaped holes were made along the edges with an awl. The women used tree roots, softened and split, for the sewing. Small openings around the stitches were sealed off with a waterproof mixture of tree gum and fish oil. These long strips of bark were then rolled up so they could be carried easily. Such rolls were highly valued and traded between tribes.

The favored site for building a bark tipi in summer was on sandy soil close to water, with a hill nearby that allowed a view over the surrounding countryside where breezes could blow away mosquitoes and black flies. In winter, a forest site was chosen where trees gave protection from the wind.

There were many variations on the tipi. The elongated tipi might have several fire pits and serve as many as ten families. In the western subarctic, a double lean-to, combining wood and bark, was insulated with brush.

6 *lean-to of sticks, bark, brush and sod*

How the tipi was built

First, a tripod was built. Three young trees were trimmed of branches to make long poles. Two of these poles were cut to a point at the top and the other forked. The bottom ends were stuck into the ground and tilted inward to meet at the top. There the two pointed sticks were fitted into the forked one. More straight, lightweight poles were then stuck in the ground, this time to form the conical tipi shape, and leaned against the first three. Two or three feet below the top, the poles were lashed together to make a firm frame for the bark covering.

In cold weather, bark is very brittle, so it must be warmed before it can be unrolled or rolled. When flexible enough to handle, it was wrapped around the frame like a cape starting at the bottom. Each row overlapped the one below it to allow rain to run off. More poles and branches were then laid against the sides to hold the bark in place and tied at the top. In winter skins and brush might be added for insulation with a final covering of snow.

Smoke from the fire escaped directly upward through the open peak. An opening left on one side as a door was covered by a flap of animal skin. Sometimes a tunnel entrance of brush and branches was added as a windbreak.

basic bark tipi

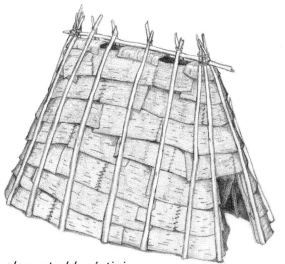

elongated bark tipi

The tipi, small and quickly built, sheltered Indian tribes who lived by hunting.

9

Bark, light to carry and easy to use, was unrolled around poles around a firepit.

The wigwam

The wigwam was a larger type of bark shelter. Although the word was used for many shapes, a true wigwam was domed, like an igloo. And like the igloo it used heat and building materials efficiently. The dome kept the heat close to the ground where people sat or slept. It also made the wigwam roomier inside than the tipi because the walls did not tilt inward as steeply.

A fire burned in a shallow pit in the center and the smoke escaped through an opening at the top of the dome. In bad weather this was closed off with a flap of bark attached to a long pole. The flap could be moved into different positions, depending on which way the wind was blowing. This kept the smoke from drifting back inside.

The wigwam was usually built to be lived in for a much longer time than the tipi by tribes that did not depend entirely on hunting and fishing for their food. Where they were able to grow corn or other grains, they could stay as long as the land was fertile, and it was not unusual to find fifty or even a hundred wigwams clustered together into a village. Since disputes over territory or trade broke out between the tribes from time to time, such villages were usually surrounded by stockades.

The tools used by the Indians, made of stone and bone, look very crude to the modern eye. Yet these axes, chisels and knives were highly efficient instruments. When Samuel de Champlain watched Indians building forts in the early 1600s he was impressed at the ease and speed with which the tools were used. Modern scientists too have been surprised when they tried using stone knives excavated from Indian sites; they found them to be sharp, fit comfortably into the hand, and, in some ways, to be better than metal knives.

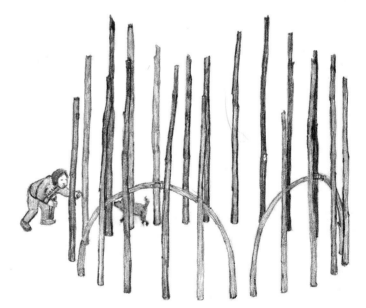

three stages of building a wigwam

How the wigwam was built

The wigwam was more difficult to build than the simple bark tipi.

Sixteen to twenty long poles were planted in the ground in a circle about fifteen feet (four and a half meters) across. They were arranged so that each pole had a mate on the opposite side of the circle. These pairs were then bent towards each other and lashed together with strips of basswood or cedar bark to form arches. Next, two or three rings of saplings were tied around the structure to increase its strength.

To cover the outside, the Indians used whatever was available: bark, animal hides, even rush mats made of cattails ingeniously sewn together to make them watertight. In cold weather all of these might be combined on the same wigwam. Bark might be layered over an inside shell of mats, and then banked with leaves, green branches or snow. For the bark roof, birch was best, being light and flexible, but chestnut, oak and elm were also used.

Sometimes a foot-high platform was built around the fire pit. This platform was spread with mats and soft skins to make a warm, comfortable place for sitting or sleeping. Wigwam walls in the more permanent settlements were lined with decorated mats. Like the bark tipi, the wigwam had an earthen floor covered with fir boughs that gave off a lovely scent. Skin or fur might be thrown over the branches for warmth.

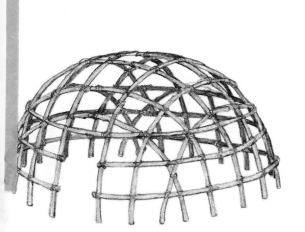

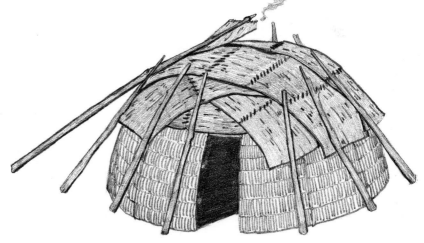

11

The wigwam – harder to build, roomier and more permanent than the tipi –

resembled the igloo in shape and efficiency. Fifty or more might make a village.

The people of the longhouse

The Iroquois of New York State called themselves "People of the Longhouse." Between 1350 and 1450, they built some of the biggest and most spectacular longhouses known. Five, then six nations united to form the Iroquoian Confederation. Other Iroquois nations did the same in southern Ontario and Quebec. They developed a form of government to maintain peace among themselves and kept simple records of treaties and trade ties. Their agriculture became more advanced and their villages more settled. Small beads made of shells called "wampum" were woven into sashes and used as a medium of exchange.

Women had considerable status among the Iroquois. Each longhouse was governed by a "matron" who might represent as many as twenty families in the one shelter. She and other matrons selected a chief to speak for the household at council meetings. Children took their mother's clan name and belonged to two families.

Their "fireside" family consisted of their parents and brothers and sisters, all living together in their section of the longhouse. The other family was made up of their mother's sisters and their children, and sometimes even of their grandmother's sisters and children. All the young children of these women were treated like brothers and sisters. This second family supervised the children's upbringing. Family members related to the fathers might live in the same settlement as well.

When the first French explorers sailed up the Saint Lawrence River in 1535 they found a huge flourishing Iroquois settlement where Montreal stands today. This village of Hochelaga was protected by three rings of walls thirty feet (nine meters) high — as high as the walls of most European fortresses of the time. Inside were some fifty very large bark longhouses centered around a meeting place, where ceremonies were performed and festivals celebrated. Outside the walls were fields of corn, beans and squash.

14 *stone ax*

A century later Champlain describes a longhouse community he visited in southeastern Ontario: "Their cabins are a kind of arbor or bower, covered with bark, approximately fifty or sixty yards long by twelve wide (fifty meters by ten meters) with a passage ten or twelve feet broad (three meters) down the middle from one end to the other. Along each side runs a bench four feet above ground, where the inmates sleep in summer to avoid the innumerable fleas. In winter they sleep close to the fire on mats, underneath the benches where it is warmer; and they fill the hut with a supply of dry wood to burn in that season. A space is left at one end of the cabin for storing their maize, which they place in large bark barrels in the middle of the floor; and boards suspended overhead preserve their clothing, food, and other things from the numerous mice. There will be a dozen fires to each cabin, making two dozen families. The smoke circulates at will, causing much eye trouble, to which the natives are so subject that many become blind in their old age. For there is no window in the cabin, and no opening except a place in the roof where the smoke finds an outlet."

palisades

garbage area

cornfields

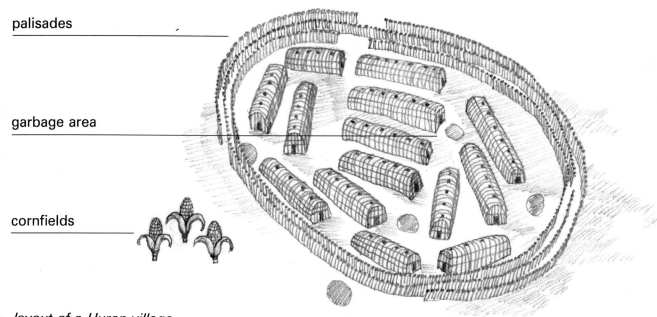

layout of a Huron village

The longhouse – largest of bark dwellings – sheltered extended families

for ten or fifteen years, as long as the surrounding farm soil remained fertile.

The longhouse

Longhouses were sometimes longer than a football field. Even when they were much smaller, building them was an architectural feat that involved many family groups, sometimes the whole community.

The longhouse might vary in length, but it was usually as high as it was wide. Posts about the thickness of a man's leg were set in two rows to form the outer frame. Then horizontal beams were stretched from one wall to another and lashed into place.

The roof frame was made of lighter poles, about as thick as a man's arm. It might be arched or come to a point at the center supported by a mast-like pole.

The whole structure was then covered with bark: usually cedar, ash or elm, because birch was not so common in southern areas. The bark was put on like shingles, from the bottom up to let water run off, as in the tipi and wigwam. Another set of poles was then lashed over the bark to keep it from blowing away. The longhouse had no windows, only doors at both ends and a row of smoke holes down the center of the roof.

Each of the related families in a longhouse had its own space along one wall, about thirteen feet (about four meters) long. A cooking fire in the center aisle was shared with the family opposite. Some longhouses also had larger fire pits for winter heating. In the biggest longhouses, three platforms ran like shelves along both walls, one above the other. They had many uses: for working and sleeping; for storing food, clothes, firewood, tools and weapons. In the wide center aisle, people cooked, ate and chatted, squinting against the smoke.

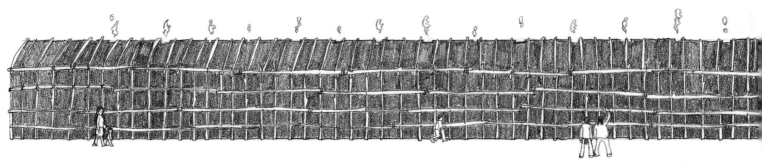

One of the largest longhouses ever found was built in New York State in A.D. 1410 and measured 400 feet

Some longhouses must have been very handsome. Walls outside the front were decorated with red and black pictures of birds, men and beasts. They might show the totem, or symbol, of the clan that dwelt inside. When a stranger entered a village, he went to the longhouse identified with his mother's clan. He could count on a warm welcome even among distant relatives.

The longhouse was less crowded in summer when men and boys hunted and fished while the women and small children tended crops and lived in small shelters in the fields. Because plowing was unknown, the soil around the village lost its fertility after ten or fifteen years of planting and families had to move. The site of their new village would already have been chosen a few years earlier. Trees were burned down and stumps dug up to clear the earth. Then a clean new longhouse was built and whatever was still useful was moved from the old home.

The longhouse was not a perfect shelter. Villages had communal garbage dumps, but years of close living meant that dirt, vermin and insects accumulated inside. In rainy weather smoke holes had to be at least partly covered and the inhabitants sometimes had to lie down to avoid the smoke.

The arrival of Europeans meant the days of the longhouse were numbered. For all its value as a building material, bark had serious drawbacks. It was flammable and fragile. It could withstand neither the heat nor the firepower of the new weapons the invaders brought. But for centuries before their arrival the bark longhouse had been one of the largest and most impressive native structures north of Mexico.

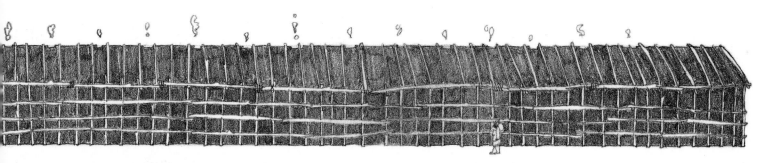

in length (125 meters). This drawing shows its size in relation to people.

Each family had its own space on the platform shelves along longhouse walls.

Other uses of bark

Bark was not just a building material. It had many uses. The birchbark canoe was perfected by Northern tribes. It is hard to match for simplicity, lightness and efficiency. Two men and four women could build one in about twelve days that would be big enough to carry a family of five or six and all their belongings swiftly over lakes and rivers.

The Iroquois shaped bark into huge grain containers that could be four feet (a little over a meter) high and three feet (one meter) wide. They could also bend and sew it into simple containers such as troughs for collecting maple sap. These might be decorated with porcupine quills and moose hair; beautiful designs were created by scraping away one layer of the bark to expose a different shade. Bark was even made into kettles for cooking, though great care had to be taken to keep it away from direct flame.

Bark could splint a broken leg. It could be dried and rolled to make an excellent torch. It could shroud the dead. Rope was made from its fibers. The inner bark of the basswood tree was boiled soft with wood ash; then it was shaved down to a strip that was a good width for weaving. Carrying bags were made of these strips. Bark could be fashioned into temporary raincoats or folded into drinking cups. The Indians also brewed a bark tea that is reported to have cured Jacques Cartier's crew of sickness.

Bark was one of the most valuable products found in nature and the many uses developed for it indicate the resourcefulness of those who once inhabited this continent.

birchbark canoe

birchbark baby carrier

23

Few bark houses are built today unless for museums.
The great longhouses are now only a dim memory.
But sites continue to be excavated telling us more
about the remarkable Indian tribes that built them.

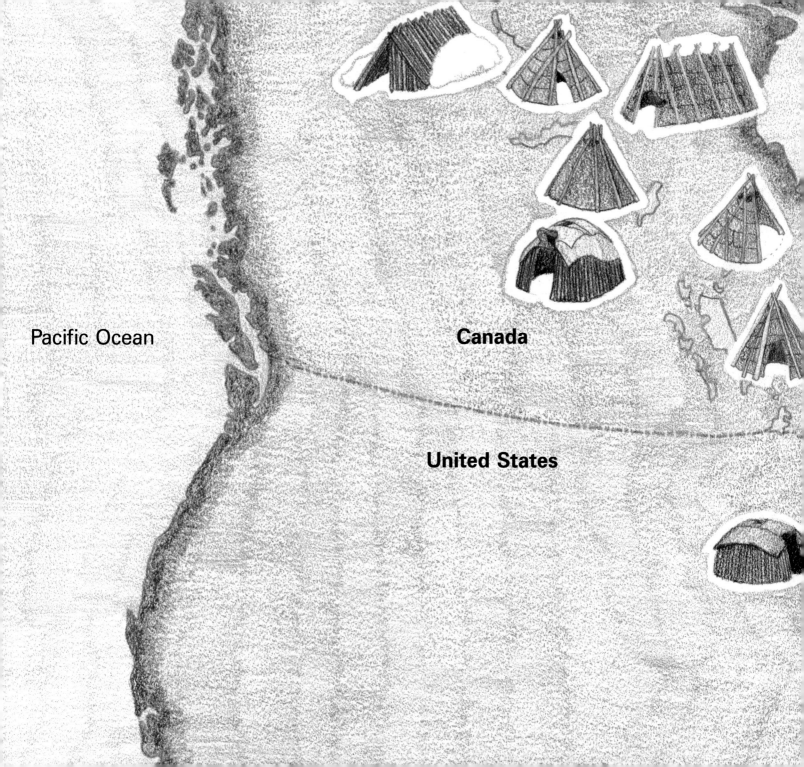

Pacific Ocean

Canada

United States

Hudson Bay

Atlantic Ocean

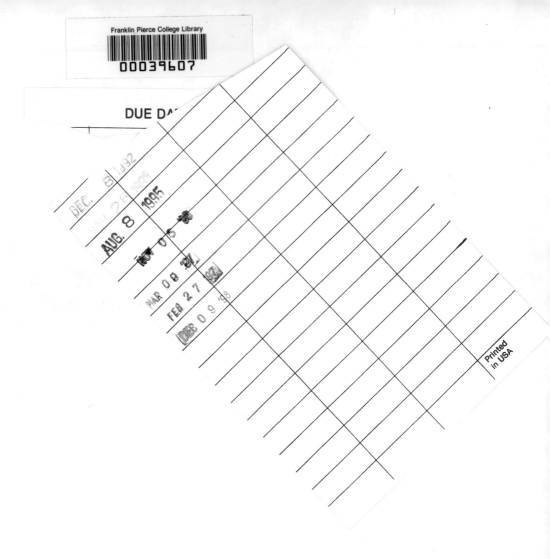

DUE DA